Getting To Know...

Nature's Children

MOUNTAIN GOATS

Bill Ivy

PUBLISHER	Joseph R. DeVarennes
PUBLICATION DIRECTOR	Kenneth H. Pearson
MANAGING EDITOR	Valerie Wyatt
SERIES ADVISOR	Merebeth Switzer
SERIES CONSULTANT	Michael Singleton
CONSULTANTS	Ross James
	Kay McKeever
	Dr. Audrey N. Tomera
ADVISORS	Roger Aubin
	Robert Furlonger
	Gaston Lavoie
EDITORIAL SUPERVISOR	Jocelyn Smyth
PRODUCTION MANAGER	Ernest Homewood
PRODUCTION ASSISTANTS	Penelope Moir
	Brock Piper

EDITORS

Katherine Farris	Anne Minguet-Patocka
Sandra Gulland	Sarah Reid
Cristel Kleitsch	Cathy Ripley
Elizabeth MacLeod	Eleanor Tourtel
Pamela Martin	Karin Velcheff

PHOTO EDITORS	Bill Ivy
DESIGN	Annette Tatchell
CARTOGRAPHER	Jane Davie
PUBLICATION ADMINISTRATION	Kathy Kishimoto

ARTISTS

Marianne Collins	Greg Ruhl
Pat Ivy	Mary Theberge

This series is approved and recommended by the Federation of Ontario Naturalists.

Canadian Cataloguing in Publication Data

Ivy, Bill, 1953–
  Moths; Mountain goats

(Getting to know—nature's children)
Issued also in French under title: Les papillons nocturnes; La chèvre de montagne.
Includes index.
ISBN 0-7172-1622-5

1. Moths—Juvenile literature.
2. Rocky Mountain goat—juvenile literature.
I. Title. II. Title: Mountain goats.   III. Series.

QL544.2.I88 1987   j595.78'1   C87-094651-X

Have you ever wondered . . .

Have you ever wished you could climb a high mountain? The icy winds and jagged cliffs are a challenge only a few people are brave enough to meet. It takes a lot of training, skill and equipment to scale the peak. Even with all that, however, the most expert mountaineer is no match for the incredible Mountain Goat. This nimble-footed animal moves with ease through remote mountain terrain where one slip up could send it tumbling to its death.

Until recently, very little was known about the Mountain Goat since it inhabits such remote areas. Read along and discover what we now know about these adventurous creatures.

Kidding Around

Like all children, young Mountain Goats, or kids, love to play. They are very frisky and will spend hours chasing each other, scrambling up rocks and jumping off, or racing up to the edge of a steep bank and stopping just in time to avoid falling over. Now and then, they pause to nibble on a few blades of grass or a tasty mountain bluebell. When at last they have tired themselves out, they drift back to snuggle down and rest beside their mothers, who have been keeping a close watch over them.

Life is not all fun and games, however. There are lessons to be learned. By following their mothers up craggy cliffs and along dangerous ledges, the kids soon become skilled little mountaineers.

I'm the king of the castle!

Head in the Clouds

Mountain Goats are found in the mountainous regions of western North America, as far north as Alaska and south to the states of Oregon and Idaho. They make their home in some of the world's most rugged terrain and generally settle close to the timberline, often as high as 2500 metres (8 000 feet) above sea level. During the winter they move to slightly lower elevations. Mountain Goats do not usually have much company, since few other animals can survive in this snowy land among the clouds!

The shaded area on this map shows where Mountain Goats live.

Kinfolk

When is a goat not a goat? When it is a Mountain Goat!

Despite its name, the Mountain Goat is not really a goat at all but is actually more closely related to the antelope family. Its closest relatives are a small group of mountain antelopes—the serow and goral of Asia and the chamois of the European Alps.

Many people confuse the Mountain Goat with the Dall's Sheep, the only other large, white mammal found in the mountains. From a distance they may look similar, but they are not related and they inhabit different areas. There is no other animal quite like the Mountain Goat in North America.

Even Mountain Goats enjoy a nice bath—a dust bath that is!

Woolly Wardrobe

The Mountain Goat is well dressed for its life in the mountains. It wears a heavy, white fleecy coat which keeps it snug and warm regardless of the weather. The shaggy outer layer is made up of guard hairs that may be up to 15 centimetres (6 inches) long and that shed both water and snow. Underneath are as much as 9 centimetres (3 to 4 inches) of very fine wool. This lovely soft undercoat helps to keep the Mountain Goat's valuable body heat from escaping.

The Indians of North America's northwest coast once used the woolly undercoat of the Mountain Goat for making their beautiful Chilkat blankets. These blankets were well known for being both lightweight and warm.

No matter how cold the wind, it cannot penetrate these warm woollies.

Hill Billies and Nannies

While the Mountain Goat may not be a goat, it certainly looks like one. It is much more stocky and heavy, however, than the familiar domestic goat. The males, known as billies, can weigh 113 kilograms (250 pounds) or more and may stand over 110 centimetres (43 inches) at the shoulder. Females, or nannies, are much lighter and shorter.

Both the nannies and the billies have beards and slender black horns. The billies' horns are gently curved while those of the nannies are straighter and curve sharply at the tips. Unlike the antlers of deer or moose, a Mountain Goat's horns will never fall off. They appear very soon after the Mountain Goat is born and continue to grow a little longer each year.

Mountain Goats walk very stiffly, and this gives them an air of dignity. In truth, their noble strut is due to their short front legs rather than their position in life.

One look at this goat's horns tells you that she's a nanny.

Amazing Feet

When it comes to climbing, the Mountain Goat is in a class of its own. It travels with complete confidence along ledges so narrow that it seems to be walking on air. Even rock faces that seem to us to go straight up are climbed with ease. How does the Mountain Goat accomplish these astonishing feats?

For one thing it has a very cool head and obviously it is not afraid of heights. It also has an amazing sense of balance. But, the real secret lies in the design of its feet. The Mountain Goat's hoofs have a hard outer edge for cutting into rock or ice. The center is filled with a soft rubber pad that gives traction. In addition the sole of each foot is slightly hollowed and acts something like a suction cup when pressed down.

Unlike a horse's hoof, which is all in one piece, the Mountain Goat's hoof is split into two "toes." These can be spread wide to prevent the animal from slipping when traveling downhill. Two claws higher up the foot serve as brakes should the goat begin to slide.

The underside of a Mountain Goat's hoof.

16

Amazing Feats

Years ago it was believed that if a Mountain Goat fell off a cliff it would land on its horns and bounce back up unharmed. Although this is certainly a tall tale, the Mountain Goat is in fact capable of feats that would make a circus performer envious!

Should one of these agile mountaineers run out of room on a ledge, it can either back up or rise up on its hind legs, turn right around and drop down safely on all fours. Moreover, it can jump from one bit of ledge to another, covering as much as 3 metres (10 feet) in a single bound.

And if a Mountain Goat wants to move to a higher ledge, it can leap straight up and hook its front feet over the top of the rock—much as you might do with your arms. With help from its back legs, it then pulls itself up over the ridge to the top. Not bad for a heavyweight!

Even the best of us make mistakes, however, and Mountain Goats are no exception. Sadly, one will on occasion lose its footing and fall to its death.

Opposite page:
Only the surefooted travel here.

Super Senses

It is almost impossible to sneak up on a
Mountain Goat. Its dark round eyes are
blackbird sharp and can spot movement at least
1500 metres (1 mile) away! In order to get a
better view of its surroundings, the Mountain
Goat has the curious habit of sitting on its
haunches the way a dog does.

Strangely the Mountain Goat is not as aware
of motion when approached from above.
However, its keen sense of smell usually detects
an enemy long before there is any danger.
Should the scent be lost in shifting breezes, the
goat still has its sensitive ears to warn it. Believe
it or not, an experienced adult has such
well-developed hearing that it can tell the
difference between rocks falling naturally and
those dropping because of an approaching
intruder.

Who goes there?

Mountain Menaces

High in its alpine home, the Mountain Goat is usually safe from enemies. Few animals dare venture into such rough territory. While a golden eagle may swoop down from the sky and snatch away a very young Mountain Goat, only the cougar and the lynx are surefooted enough to be a threat on the ground. And even these predators are rarely able to get close enough to strike.

Should the Mountain Goat move into the valleys for food, however, it is in much more danger. In these areas, grizzly bears, coyotes, wolves and wolverines may also attack.

When threatened the Mountain Goat knows how to defend itself. Few animals are brave—or foolish—enough to take on its dagger-sharp horns, and those that have done so have ended up the worse for the encounter.

Of much greater danger to the goat are rock slides and avalanches. Several members of a herd can be buried should the snow on a mountainside give way. In fact, more Mountain Goats die this way than by any other means.

Opposite page:

No one is going to get my goat!

22

Slim Pickin's

In the harsh land of the Mountain Goat, food is often hard to find. Still Mountain Goats somehow manage to find enough plants to keep themselves alive. Grasses, sedges and rushes make up the bulk of their diet, but they also browse on trees and shrubs whenever they get the chance. Although they feed throughout the day, their main meals are breakfast and dinner.

Do you like the taste of salt? Well, Mountain Goats certainly do. They will travel great distances just to visit a natural salt lick. How about the taste of clay? That's right. Clay! Believe it or not, Mountain Goats like to snack on a special type of clay that is found high in the mountains. Using their sharp teeth, they nip off chunks of this earthy meal and chew it up as you would a carrot.

The Mountain Goat's strong, sharp teeth are ideal for snipping off tasty twigs.

Overleaf:
Enjoying a cool refreshing drink.

Leftovers Again!

What do deer, cows and Mountain Goats have in common? They all eat first and chew later.

Instead of chewing its food well before swallowing, the Mountain Goat gulps down its meal almost whole. The unchewed food is stored in a special part of the animal's stomach. Then when the goat feels like relaxing, it brings this food back up into its mouth and chews it at its leisure. This is known as "chewing the cud." Once the goat has done all the chewing it wants, the cud is once again swallowed for digestion in another part of the stomach.

Chewing the cud.

Mountain Bands

In Mountain Goat society, the nannies are the bosses (except during the mating season). Most billies live alone or in small loose groups during the summer, then join up with the females and their young. They soon learn their place as the high-ranking females keep them in line with their sharp horns.

The males, females and young Mountain Goats live together through the winter in bands of up to 20 members. While the herd is feeding, a sentinel stands guard, and keeps a close watch for any sign of danger.

The band does not usually travel very far. Its home range is often no more than 8 kilometres (5 miles). The goats spend a lot of time lying down in shallow depressions which they scoop out of the rock or ground.

Get Your Goat

Whenever they meet, billies usually get along fairly well—that is until the mating season, which occurs in late fall. Then they start bickering over whose nanny is whose.

Should two males want the same female, things may get rather tense. The angry billies stand head to tail daring each other to make a move. They arch their backs and stand tall, and if one of them does not give in, they might come to blows. Using their horns as daggers these white knights lunge sideways at each other. Usually the fighting does not last long, but it can become quite violent and result in serious injuries. Luckily, few battles actually take place.

The victorious males have a peculiar way of impressing the nannies. They crawl on their bellies and bleat like lambs. Don't laugh, it works!

A big billie.

Nanny's Nursery

In late spring, the nanny gives birth. For a nursery she selects a sheltered spot such as a cave or grassy ledge on a cliff. Usually one baby, or kid, is born but twins are not uncommon. On rare occasions triplets surprise their mother.

Immediately after the kid is born the nanny licks its wet, woolly coat dry. Unlike its mother, the newborn Mountain Goat may have prominent streaks of brown hair down its back. On top of its head are two black leathery spots where horns will soon grow.

Within minutes of its birth, the trembling kid struggles to its feet and soon begins to feed on its mother's milk. As it nurses it wags its stubby tail just like a barnyard goat. Only 33 centimetres (13 inches) tall at the shoulder and weighing about 3 kilograms (7 pounds), the newborn kid grows stronger every minute.

Keeping close to Mom.

New Kid on the Block

In less than an hour the wide-eyed kid is hopping around on its stilty legs. It follows its mother very closely, bleating softly whenever it wants to nurse. The nanny is careful to keep her baby hidden among the rocks whenever she wanders out to feed. She never stays away too long since the kid is totally dependent on her for food and protection.

At the first sign of danger the young goat will either drop to the ground and freeze or scramble beneath its mother. Any animal that might want to harm the kid must get by the nanny first! After a few days the mother and her kid come out of isolation and join the band of other nannies and their young.

When only one week old the kids begin to nibble on vegetation, but they will continue to drink their mother's milk for another five weeks or so. They grow quickly and by winter they weigh about 10 kilograms (22 pounds).

The young will stay with their mothers through the winter, but come spring, the nannies will send them off on their own before the new kids are born.

The rejected youngsters do not go very far, however. Most continue to "hang around" with the band for at least another year.

These kids' horns are already growing. By winter they will be about 9 centimetres (3-1/2 inches) long.

Hard Times

Winter in Mountain Goat country is extremely harsh. It is hard to believe that any creature could survive the freezing temperature and deep snowfalls. Yet the hardy Mountain Goats manage to endure the worst that this season has to offer. Staying warm is not really a problem as their extra-thick coats keep them cozy and dry. During particularly bad storms the goats may take shelter in a cave or beneath a rock ledge.

Mountain Goats often abandon the uppermost part of their range in the wintertime.

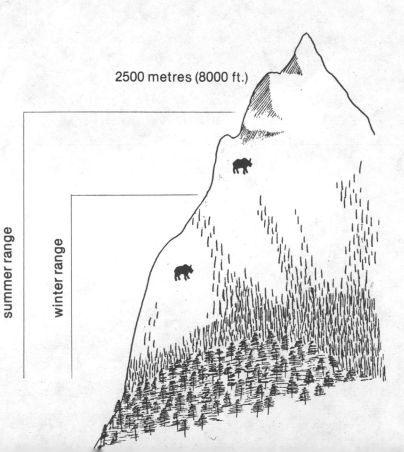

2500 metres (8000 ft.)

summer range

winter range

On the other hand, finding enough food to eat can be difficult in this winter wonderland. Should the snow become too deep to paw through, the goats will move to lower altitudes and settle on steeper, windblown slopes where the snow is not so deep and the plants are more exposed.

Even in these areas, food is never plentiful at this time of the year, and the Mountain Goats will not get much more than they need to keep alive. One result is that their horns grow more slowly, forming a narrower growth ring between those that form over the rest of the year. By counting these narrow rings as you would those of a trcc trunk, you can tell the number of winters the goat has lived. The average Mountain Goat lives about ten rings.

Overleaf:

Explorer Captain James Cook reported seeing polar bears high on the cliffs when he visited North America. What he probably saw were these monarchs of the mountains.

Change of Clothes

When the first warm weather of spring arrives, it is time for the Mountain Goat to change out of its heavy winter coat into something a little more comfortable. Gradually, over the next couple of months, its fleece begins to thin out. Large patches of it are shed and catch on rocks and bushes.

At this stage, the Mountain Goat looks very scraggly, with many clumps of wool hanging from its body. However, before too long, a new lightweight summer coat grows in. This outfit gradually begins to thicken in the fall. New guard hairs grow and a thick undercoat develops just in time for the next long cold winter.

Caught changing!

Goat Watching

Unless you are willing to do a lot of climbing you will probably never see a Mountain Goat up close. A good pair of binoculars are a must for the serious goat watcher. Today, the majority of Mountain Goats are found in government parks. Even so, there are not that many of them living in the wild, so consider yourself lucky if you do happen to see one.

Who knows, perhaps you will one day be adventurous enough to visit these beautiful beasts in their natural environment and see first hand some of the things you have just read about.

The underside of a Mountain Goat's hoof.

Some Mountain Goats are as curious about us as we are about them.

Special Words

Avalanche   A mass of snow, rock and ice that runs down a mountain quickly and suddenly.

Band   A group of Mountain Goats.

Billy   A male Mountain Goat.

Browse   Feed on.

Cud   Hastily swallowed food brought back for chewing by cud chewers such as deer, cows and Mountain Goats.

Guard hairs   Long coarse hairs that make up the outer layer of the Mountain Goat's coat.

Kid   A young Mountain Goat.

Mating season   The time of year during which animals come together to produce young.

Nanny   A female Mountain Goat.

Nurse   To drink the mother's milk.

Predator   An animal that hunts other animals for food.

Sedge   Grass-like plant.

Sentinel   A guard that watches for danger and signals alarm if necessary.

Timberline   The point of elevation in mountainous regions beyond which no trees grow.

INDEX

Cover Photo: T.W. Hall, Environment Canada.
Photo Credits: Brian Milne (First Light), pages 4, 14, 20, 24, 46; Thomas Kitchen, pages 8, 13, 17, 37, 44; Thomas Kitchen (Valan), page 7; Esther Schmidt (Valan), pages 11, 23; Pat Morrow (First Light), page 18; Dennis A. Schmidt (Valan), pages 26-27, 31, 34; Albert Kuhnick (First Light), pages 28, 40; Halle Flygare (Valan), page 33; Robert C. Simpson (Valan), page 43.

Printed and Bound in Spain

Getting To Know...

Nature's Children

MOTHS

Bill Ivy

PUBLISHER	Joseph R. DeVarennes
PUBLICATION DIRECTOR	Kenneth H. Pearson
MANAGING EDITOR	Valerie Wyatt
SERIES ADVISOR	Merebeth Switzer
SERIES CONSULTANT	Michael Singleton
CONSULTANTS	Ross James
	Kay McKeever
	Dr. Audrey N. Toméra
ADVISORS	Roger Aubin
	Robert Furlonger
	Gaston Lavoie
EDITORIAL SUPERVISOR	Jocelyn Smyth
PRODUCTION MANAGER	Ernest Homewood
PRODUCTION ASSISTANTS	Penelope Moir
	Brock Piper

EDITORS

Katherine Farris	Anne Minguet-Patocka
Sandra Gulland	Sarah Reid
Cristel Kleitsch	Cathy Ripley
Elizabeth MacLeod	Eleanor Tourtel
Pamela Martin	Karin Velcheff

PHOTO EDITORS	Bill Ivy
DESIGN	Annette Tatchell
CARTOGRAPHER	Jane Davie
PUBLICATION ADMINISTRATION	Kathy Kishimoto

ARTISTS

Marianne Collins	Greg Ruhl
Pat Ivy	Mary Theberge

This series is approved and recommended by the Federation of Ontario Naturalists.

Canadian Cataloguing in Publication Data

Ivy, Bill, 1953–
  Moths; Mountain goats

(Getting to know—nature's children)
Issued also in French under title: Les papillons nocturnes; La chèvre de montagne.
Includes index.
ISBN 0-7172-1622-5

1. Moths—Juvenile literature.
2. Rocky Mountain goat—juvenile literature.
I. Title.   II. Title: Mountain goats.   III. Series.

QL544.2.I88 1987   j595.78'1   C87-094651-X

Have you ever wondered . . .

When someone mentions the word *moth,* what comes to mind? If you are like most people, you probably think of a drab little insect that is about as exciting as a slug! But did you know that many moths are as graceful and beautiful as butterflies? Even those that seem dull at first glance are often exquisitely patterned when seen up close.

Moths come in all sizes, shapes and colors. Some have a wingspan larger than your hand while others are so tiny that you can barely see them. The one thing they all have in common is that their life story is one of the most fascinating in nature. So if you have always thought of moths as boring, you are in for a surprise! Curious? Then read on.

The exquisite Luna Moth is found only in North America and is this continent's only swallow-tailed moth.

Where They Live

There are very few places in the world where moths do not live. They can be found in fields and woods, in scorching hot deserts and on cool mountain slopes. In North America alone there may be 15 000 different species! No one knows the exact number since new species are constantly being discovered.

Although moths far outnumber their more popular cousins, the butterflies, they are not as well known since most of them are creatures of the night.

The Pale Beauty Moth can be found all across Canada and in many parts of the United States.

Who's Who?

Have you ever wondered how you can tell the difference between a moth and a butterfly? Although it is not always easy to tell them apart, here are a few clues to help you:

— Most moths are active between dusk and dawn, while butterflies are only active during the day.

— While at rest, moths generally fold their wings flat over their backs; butterflies usually hold theirs upright and shut tight.

— Butterflies have a club at the tip of their antennae, while moths have feathery or thread-like antennae.

— Finally, moths have thicker, furrier bodies than butterflies and most of them are not as colorful.

The Ctenucha Moth can be found on grasses and flowers during the day.

Moths Up Close

Moths, like all insects, have six legs and three body parts: the head, thorax and abdomen. Most have two pairs of wings which are covered with millions of tiny colored scales. This is why moths—like their butterfly relatives—belong to a group of insects known as *Lepidoptera,* a Greek word which means "scaly winged."

The scales on a moth's wing overlap each other like the shingles on a roof and rub off as a fine dust if you touch them. They provide the wings with their colors and patterns and protect them from damage.

When the Io Moth opens its wings, two large eyespots appear. It is thought that these markings may frighten away enemies interested in a moth dinner.

Super Sight

The world must look quite different to moths than it does to us. Like all insects, a moth has not one but two sets of eyes. Most important are the two enormous *compound* eyes, made up of thousands of tiny, six-sided lenses. Under a microscope these strange eyes look like a honeycomb. Then, hidden in the hair behind the moth's feelers is a set of two small, simple eyes. No wonder moths have such excellent eyesight and can detect the slightest movement!

Again like other insects—and like us—moths can see in color. In fact, their eyes are sensitive to a color that we are unable to see—ultraviolet. Seeing ultraviolet is like adding bright orange to a gray picture. Ultraviolet is much more visible at night than most colors and many of the flowers moths feed on reflect it. The ability to see it is therefore very useful to moths since most of them feed at night.

The Promethea Moth is one of the few species in which the males and females do not look alike. This female is much more colorful than her blackish mate.

Other Senses

A moth's antennae act as a nose and are very sensitive to odors. This keen sense of smell helps moths find food, but probably its most important use is to help male moths find a mate. Female moths give off a scent that the males find irresistible. Some suitors can detect this perfume several kilometres (miles) away!

In a different way, a moth's sense of taste is as remarkable as its sense of smell: it is located in the soles of the moth's feet! By walking on a blossom, moths can immediately tell whether or not there is nectar inside. If so, they simply uncoil their long tube-like "tongue" and drink up!

Many moths can also hear. Using round drum-like membranes on their bodies, they can detect a variety of sounds including some of the high-pitched squeaks of a hunting bat. Incredibly, some moths seem to be able to imitate the bat's sounds. This confuses it and allows the moth to escape.

Opposite page:
If there is a female close by, these fern-like antennae will help this male Cecropia Moth track her down.

Fatal Attraction

Have you ever heard the expression, "like a moth to a flame?" It means to be irresistibly drawn to something, as moths are to light. Often, you can see large swarms of moths fluttering aimlessly around streetlights at night. What causes this strange behavior?

One theory is that moths navigate by the light of the moon. Since the moon is so far from the earth, its rays strike the ground parallel to each other. By keeping the angle of moonlight that hits its eyes the same, the moth keeps on course. However, with lights that are much closer, the rays radiate out like the spokes of a wheel. In order to keep these beams striking its eyes at the same angle, the moth must keep turning closer and closer to the light. Should this beacon happen to be a flame it's soon "lights out" for the unsuspecting moth!

This beautiful Haploa Moth is attracted to lights at night.

Small Beginnings

Like a bird, a moth begins its life as an egg. Of course, moths' eggs are much smaller than birds' eggs. Most, in fact are no bigger than the head of a pin. They come in various shapes and colors. They may be round or flat, cone- or barrel-shaped. Some are smooth while others are ribbed. Most are a plain brown, green or white color but some are spotted. In each case, the eggs are designed to blend in with their surroundings so that hungry creatures cannot find them.

When a female is ready to lay her eggs she finds a suitable spot. The majority glue their eggs either singly or in groups to the ground or onto leaves, plants, stems or bark. One female may lay as many as 10 000 eggs. Then her job is complete: she flies off and never sees her young.

Most eggs hatch within a week, but those laid in the fall may overwinter and hatch the following spring.

Cecropia Moth eggs.

Curious Cats

The first meal a newborn caterpillar, or larva, eats is often its own egg shell. The second is usually fresh leaves, although some larvae feed on fruit, seeds or wood. One species is particularly fond of apples—as you may already know if you have ever gone to bite into an apple and found yourself eye to eye with a "worm!"

The young larva has an incredible appetite and eats both day and night, stopping only for the briefest of rests. It grows very quickly and

One of our best-known caterpillars is that of the Isabella Tiger Moth, commonly known as the woolly bear. Its main claim to fame is its supposed ability to predict the weather. According to folklore the closer together the black bands are on each end of its body, the more severe the approaching winter will be. Unfortunately, the woolly bear is even less reliable at predicting the weather than our own weather forecasters.

soon it is too big for its skin. If you wear a coat
that is too small, it will finally tear at the seams
and this is what happens to the caterpillar. Its
old skin splits down the back, and the larva
crawls out wearing the new baggy skin that has
grown underneath. This is known as molting
and usually occurs five times before the
caterpillar is fully grown. Each time the
caterpillar's colors may be different and its body
may even change shape as new parts are grown
or lost.

Many caterpillars are smooth, while others
are covered with warts and bumps. Several
species are hairy. In fact, the word caterpillar
comes from a Latin name meaning "hairy cat."
All caterpillars have six legs and up to five pairs
of large claspers that they use for gripping.
Although larvae have twelve tiny eyes they can
probably only see well enough to tell light from
dark. For this reason they must rely on their two
antennae to help them find their way around.

Dangerous Lives

Life is very dangerous for moth larvae. Mice, chipmunks, frogs, snakes, spiders and birds all enjoy a meal of juicy fat caterpillars. A single pair of nesting birds may feed as many as a hundred caterpillars a day to their hungry nestlings! However, the caterpillars' most deadly enemies are the tiny wasps and flies that lay eggs on their bodies. These eggs soon hatch into tiny larvae that immediately begin to feed on their unfortunate hosts. The poor caterpillars are literally eaten alive!

Caterpillars have a variety of ways to protect themselves. A few species have poisonous hairs or spines, while others taste so bad that no animal would want to eat them. Still others have a dangerous-looking horn-like projection that they wave defiantly at intruders. Most caterpillars, however, rely on their ability to blend into their surroundings. Some are so well camouflaged that they are almost impossible to see.

Opposite page:
The amazing appetite of the Polyphemus Moth caterpillar has earned it a place in the Guinness Book of World Records. *In the first 48 hours of its life it eats about 86 000 times its own birthweight in food.*

Preparing for Change

When fully grown a moth larva stops eating and prepares for the next change of its life. It must now select a safe place to molt for the last time. Some species burrow into the ground while others crawl under loose bark, fallen leaves or rocks. Most spin strong silken cocoons around themselves for protection from enemies and bad weather. To do this, they use special glands near their mouth. Liquid silk is forced out through little nozzles known as spinnerets and quickly hardens into a slender thread.

Next, the caterpillar begins to shrink and shrivel and looks as if it is dying. When it finally sheds its skin, it is no longer a caterpillar but a strange mummy-like creature known as a pupa. The pupa's soft pale skin soon hardens and darkens. It is within this seemingly lifeless case that a miracle takes place.

The Cecropia Moth pupa spends the winter in a strong waterproof cocoon attached to a twig.

A Great Mystery

If you are every lucky enough to come across a
pupa, look carefully at the outer surface and
you will see the outline of the future moth's
wings, legs and antennae. And yet, unbelievable
as it may seem, there is nothing inside but a
milky liquid. Somehow this mysterious liquid
will gradually solidify into a fully formed moth.

Exactly how this incredible change takes
place, no one fully understands. In some kinds
of moths it takes only a few days. In others it
may take over a year.

*The word pupa means doll. Does
this Regal Moth pupa look like a
little doll wrapped in its blanket to
you?*

New Life

In order to begin its new life a moth must first break out of its cramped quarters. By expanding itself with air and tightening its muscles the moth splits its pupa shell and pulls itself out. Those in a cocoon have another barrier to break through. Some species use a built-in escape hatch. Others have special cutters that they use to clip their way to freedom. Many moths produce a fluid that dissolves the cocoon's silk fibers.

Once the moth is free it must find a safe place to hang. What a sorry looking sight it is with its damp swollen body and small crumpled wings! But then its wings begin to unfold. Gradually they expand to their full size, and the moth has only to wait for them to harden and dry before it can take to the air.

The moth has now reached its fourth and final stage and will change and grow no more. The most vital part of its life still lies ahead, however. It must now find a mate and start the whole cycle of life again.

Opposite page:
Free at last!
(Luna Moth)

Now that you know more about moths in general, let's take a closer look at a few of these fascinating insects.

Champion Flyers

Next time you see what appears to be a hummingbird darting from flower to flower, look again—it just might be a Hawk Moth. Like hummingbirds these incredible moths have extra long tongues that enable them to feed on the nectar of deep-throated flowers. Also like hummingbirds, they can hover in mid-air and can even fly backwards! With their tapered bodies and narrow wings, these streamlined insects are the fastest fliers in the moth world. Some species reach speeds of 60 kilometres (37 miles) per hour.

The Hawk Moth is also known as the Sphinx Moth because of its caterpillar's peculiar habit of resting motionless with its front end rearing up. In this pose it looks like a tiny copy of the world-famous Egyptian Sphinx.

Opposite page: *Many Hawk Moths are beautifully marked with brightly colored hindwings or large eyespots. The eyespots on this Blinded Sphinx Moth are easy to see.*

Measuring Up

Have you ever walked under a tree on a hot summer day and come face to face with a caterpillar dangling on a thread of silk? If so, you have already met the Geometer Moth's caterpillar, better known as the inchworm. Next time you see one, let it land on you and watch the curious way it moves. First it stretches its front end forward as far as it can. Next it grabs hold with its claspers and loops up the rest of its body to make both ends meet. Then it does the same thing again—and again and again and again.

If you can easily recognize Geometer Moth caterpillars by the odd way they move, how do you recognize the adults? By the way they don't move! Unlike the majority of moths, most members of this family rest with their wings spread out flat. Among the exceptions to this rule are the females of some species. Them, you recognize by the surprising fact that they do not have any wings at all!

Opposite page: *Unlike most Geometer Moths, Kent's Geometer Moth rests with its wings closed up over its back the way a butterfly does.*

Now You See Them, Now You Don't

The Underwing Moths are masters of camouflage. During the day they rest on tree trunks or rocks where they blend in so well with their surroundings that they are almost invisible. Hidden beneath their drab front wings, however, are colorful hindwings that are usually marked with bands of red, yellow, black or orange.

This eye-catching arrangement probably helps these moths live longer. In flight their underwings flash color, but once the moth lands the color suddenly disappears. Any enemy that may have been chasing one will probably fly right past in search of the bright markings. How's that for a vanishing act?

The Once-married Underwing.

35

Tiny Tigers

It is easy to see how the Tiger Moth, with its bold black and white or yellow markings, got its name. These beautiful moths live in the woods and are usually active only at night. During the day they rest on the bark of trees against which their brilliant colors are very noticeable. But doesn't that make them easy prey for hungry insectivores? Easy maybe, but not very appetizing. A captured Tiger Moth gives off an awful-smelling liquid that usually convinces its enemies to leave it alone. The brilliant color may actually serve as a warning for potential diners to look elsewhere.

Although you may never have seen a Tiger Moth, you have probably crossed paths with its caterpillar. It has a fuzzy body and is commonly seen running along the ground. If you pick it up it will roll into a ball and play dead.

Great Tiger Moth.

Night Owls

If you were to search the woods with a flashlight at night, you might find a pair of tiny eyes glowing eerily in the dark. Should this happen to you, don't be afraid. They are most likely the eyes of an Owlet Moth. Of course, you can now guess how these moths got their name. Like owls, they have eyes that shine when light strikes them, and most are active at night. At rest during the day, Owlet Moths hold their wings roof-like over their bodies, resembling tiny triangles. They are sometimes called Miller Moths because the scales on their wings rub off like fine flour.

There are more Owlet Moths in the world than any other species.

Owlet Moth caterpillars are often mistaken for worms. Most pupate in the ground and take up to two years to complete their life cycle. One group, known as cutworms, have the annoying habit of nipping off tender plant shoots at night. Needless to say, they are not very popular with gardeners!

Opposite page: *The tiny 8-spotted Forester Moth is one of our most beautiful Owlet Moths.*

Winged Royalty

Meet the grandest family of the moth world, the Silk or Emperor Moths. These royal creatures are among our largest and most beautiful insects. Not only is their size impressive—some have a wingspan of over 15 centimetres (6 inches)—but their wings are works of art. Many have a transparent window in the middle of each hindwing and display large "peacock eyes" that seem to stare right at you. Their bodies are stocky and covered with thick hair. In flight, Silk Moths are often mistaken for bats.

If you have never seen a Silk Moth before, there is a good reason why. Not only are most species active only at night, but they have a very short lifespan. They do not eat once they become adults so that they can put all their time and energy into finding a mate, seeking out the right kind of tree and laying their eggs on it. They live only long enough to complete these tasks—usually one or two weeks.

Opposite page:
The Polyphemus Moth is named after the one-eyed Cyclops of Greek mythology. Why? Its large eyespots are the obvious answer.

A Taste for Trouble

While moths are generally harmless, the larvae of a few species can be a pest, especially those that eat the same foods as we do! Some burrow into fruit such as apples and peaches, while others attack fields of corn, grain and cotton. No less a problem are those that strip leaves off trees and plants. When they occur in large numbers, they can cause severe damage to forests.

Another common pest is known for its unusual diet. Have you ever taken a sweater out of the closet and discovered it had tiny holes in it? If so, the damage may have been the work of the Common Clothes Moth larvae, which have an appetite for wool, silk and fur. Many people mistakenly believe that the adult moths also eat clothes, but this is not true. In fact, they do not eat at all!

Many moths blend in so well with their surroundings that they are almost impossible to see. Can you spot the Hawk Moth in this picture?

Friends in Deed

Moths are not only fascinating but useful too. Many flowers that bloom at night depend upon them for survival. Plants cannot produce seeds without first being pollinated. As moths visit flowers to feed, some of the pollen rubs off the flowers onto their bodies and is carried to other plants. A few of our important crops are pollinated this way as well.

We also have the moth to thank for one of our most treasured luxuries—silk. The Silkworm Moth of Asia has been used for over 4000 years to produce this wonderful cloth. Its silk cocoon is carefully unravelled into one long strand which is then combined with other threads and woven into fabric.

Believe it or not, it takes over 50 000 cocoons to make a single kilogram (2 pounds) of silk! So if you ever have the pleasure of slipping into a silk shirt, or the next time you find a beautiful moth clinging to your window screen in the morning, consider what a poorer place this world would be without moths.

And if you are still not convinced, try discovering moths first hand. Shine a bright light on an outside wall at night and you will be amazed at the variety of moths that come. It is one of the best shows around and constantly changes as new moths emerge throughout the year.

Originally from China, the Cynthia Moth was introduced to North America as a possible silk producer.

Special Words

Antennae Sensory organs of insects, such as moths.

Camouflage Coloring that makes an animal blend into the background.

Caterpillar The second stage in a moth's life. Also called the *larva*.

Claspers The grasping hooks that a caterpillar uses to hold on to things.

Compound eyes Eyes that have many lenses instead of just one.

Cocoon A strong silk case that a caterpillar spins around itself in preparation for the next, *pupa,* stage of its life.

Eyespots Spots on the wings of some moths that look like a pair of eyes.

Gland A part of the body where certain substances are made.

Insectivores Animals that eat mainly insects.

Larva The caterpillar stage of a moth's life.

Lepidoptera The order of insects to which moths and butterflies belong.

Molt To shed old skin or feathers to make way for new.

Pupa The third stage in a moth's life during which it changes into its adult form.

Pupate To go through the pupa stage.

Spinnerets The part of the caterpillar's body that forms the silk threads with which it spins its cocoon.

Thorax The part of a moth's body, behind the head, to which the wings and the legs are attached.

INDEX

Cover Photo: Bill Ivy.
Photo Credits: All photos by Bill Ivy.

Printed and Bound in Spain